Which Way Is UP?

Which Way Is UP?

Written *by* Gail Kay Haines

Illustrated by Lisa Amoroso

ATHENEUM 1987 NEW YORK

To Mike   G. K. H.

To two special people—my mother and father.   L.A.

Atheneum
Macmillan Publishing Company
866 Third Avenue, New York, NY 10022

Type set by Linoprint Composition, New York City
Printed and bound by the Maple-Vail Book Manufacturing Group, Binghamton, N.Y.
Typography by Mary Ahern
First Edition

10 9 8 7 6 5 4 3 2 1

Library of Congress Cataloging in Publication Data

Haines, Gail Kay.
Which way is up?

SUMMARY: An explanation of gravity and the discoveries
that have been made about it—although we still don't know
exactly how it works.
1. Gravitation—Juvenile literature.   [1. Gravity]
I. Amoroso, Lisa, ill.   II. Title.
QC178.H128   1987   531'.14   86-17239
ISBN 0-689-31285-7

How do you know which way is up? By looking at the ceiling or the sky? By watching the way trees grow? By tossing a ball? What does "up" mean, anyway?

How do you know which way is down? By looking at your feet? By dropping a rock? What does "down" mean, anyway?

Close your eyes. Do you still know which way is up? How does "up" feel? Let your head hang between your knees. How does "down" feel?

Scuba divers, swimming in cloudy water, sometimes get confused. Water presses on them from all sides, and all directions begin to feel the same. When that happens, they watch their bubbles. Bubbles float up.

Mountain climbers caught in an avalanche have the same problem. Buried under heavy snow, they can't tell which way to dig. An old mountaineer's trick is to spit into the snow. Saliva sinks down, and the climber digs up.

The earth is round like a giant ball, and it feels as if we live right on top. How would it feel to live on the bottom? Would "up" still be up? How can you tell?

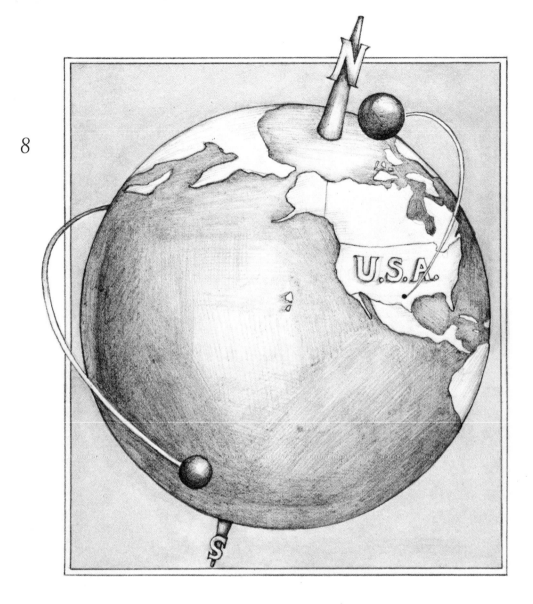

If you toss a ball at the North Pole, it goes up in the air and falls down to the ground. Toss a ball at the South Pole. Exactly the same thing happens. In China and Australia, in America and every other country, "up" points away from earth and "down" points back. "Away from earth" and "toward earth" are what "up" and "down" mean—to everyone on earth.

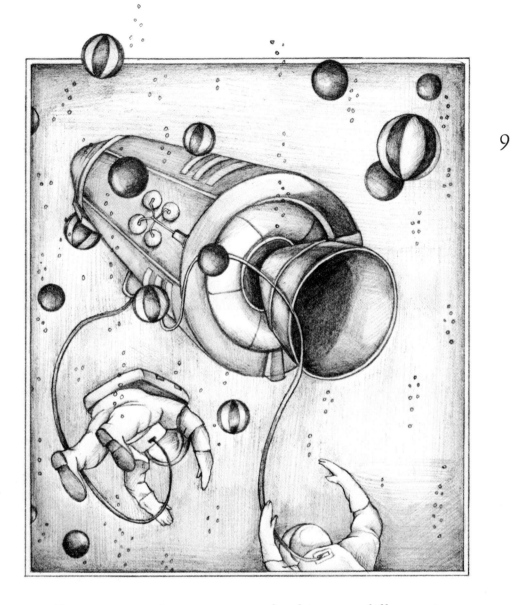

For astronauts in a space capsule, things are different. Astronauts feel as comfortable drifting one way as another. Balls and bubbles simply float around. Astronauts travel far out in space where "toward earth" and "away from earth" don't make much difference. There is no way to tell up from down in space. In fact, there *is* no up or down in space.

Gravity is the name for what makes "up" up and "down" down. Gravity causes the earth to pull everything toward itself. It works all the time. Gravity never quits.

Gravity determines how much you weigh by how hard it pulls on you. A scale simply measures how hard gravity is pulling. Gravity pulls harder on a wrestler than on a baby, so the wrestler weighs more. But in outer space, far enough away from earth's gravity, they would both weigh the same—nothing!

You are right if you think the wrestler would still be bigger than the baby. He would still have larger hands and feet and everything else. The wrestler will always have more of what scientists call "mass" than the baby. But mass is not the same thing as weight. Mass measures substance, or "stuff." Weight measures the pull of earth's gravity.

Some of the smartest scientists in the world have studied gravity. They discovered some surprises.

Which falls faster, a big rock or a small pebble? If you push both off a cliff at the same time, which hits the ground first?

About four hundred years ago, a man named Galileo Galilei decided to check. One story (which may not be true) says he dropped two metal balls, one heavy and one light, off the famous Leaning Tower in Pisa, Italy, where he lived. Both balls hit the ground at the same time.

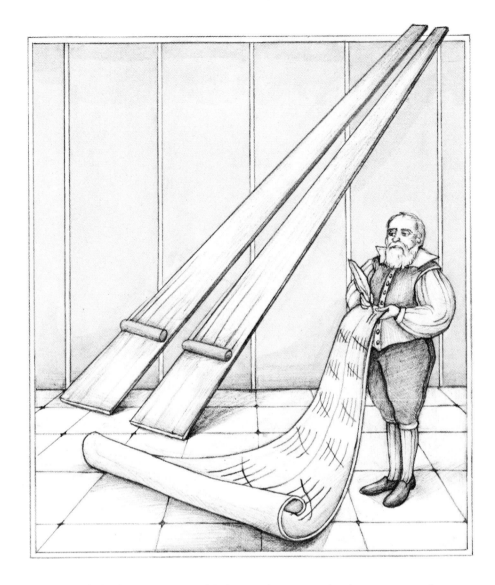

Or did they? It would have happened almost too fast to measure. Galileo needed a better way to watch gravity work.

To "slow down" gravity, Galileo decided to roll metal tubes down slanted boards. He did hundreds of experiments, and he always got the same result. Every time, a light object rolled down just as fast as a heavy one.

Galileo did not have the stopwatches scientists use today to measure small differences in time, so he made a time-counter from falling drops of water. His experiments show that the speed of gravity's pull does not depend upon what an object weighs. Things all start falling at the same speed, and the farther something falls, the faster it is moving by the time it touches earth.

Only *very* light things, such as a feather or a parachute, fall slower, because the air helps hold them up. If you could take away the air, a feather would fall as fast as a brick.

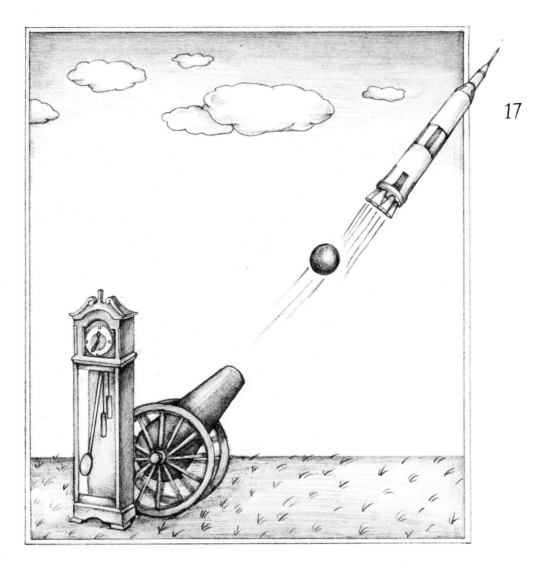

This knowledge helps people predict what falling objects will do. Scientists have used Galileo's discovery in many different ways, from inventing the clock (they can predict how fast a hanging pendulum will swing) to aiming a cannon (they know how far the cannonball will travel) to firing a space satellite (they know how far and fast it needs to fly).

Another young scientist may have been sitting under an apple tree in England, when an apple fell beside him. Maybe it hit him on the head! But Isaac Newton began to wonder if the same force that makes apples fall could also make the moon and stars move.

Starting about three hundred and fifty years ago, Isaac Newton worked out almost everything we know about gravity. He learned that every object in the universe attracts, or pulls on, every other object. That sounded wrong to most people. Everyone knows gravity doesn't make apples and people and mountains all bump into each other.

Isaac Newton explained. On small objects, gravity is a very, *very* tiny force. The force of gravity pulling a man toward a tree or a tree toward a man is so small it can be ignored. Gravity, by itself, can't move either one toward the other.

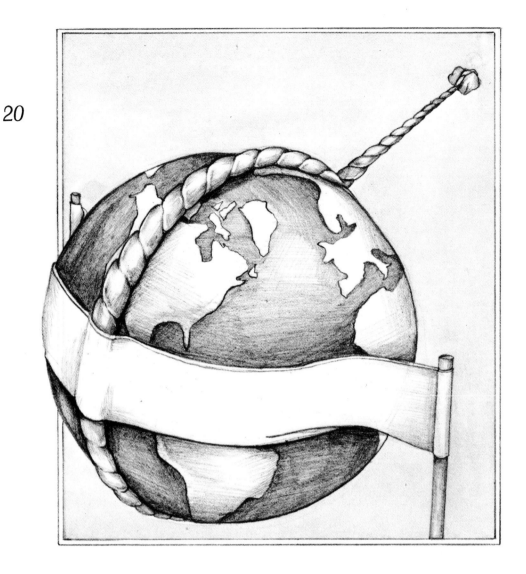

How hard gravity pulls depends upon the size of the object doing the pulling. Large objects pull much harder than small ones. And super-huge objects, such as the Earth and the sun and the stars, pull so hard on everything around them that no other forces even matter.

Gravity is a kind of tug-of-war game. Toss a rock into the air. Gravity from the rock pulls on the earth and gravity from the earth pulls on the rock. Earth wins with a thud, every time. Earth *always* wins when the "game" is played on or anywhere near earth.

The nearest object to win a tugging contest against earth is the moon. You can see the moon's gravity at work when you go to the beach. As it orbits earth, the moon (with some help from the sun) pulls hard enough on the ocean to move the water. This movement is called the tide.

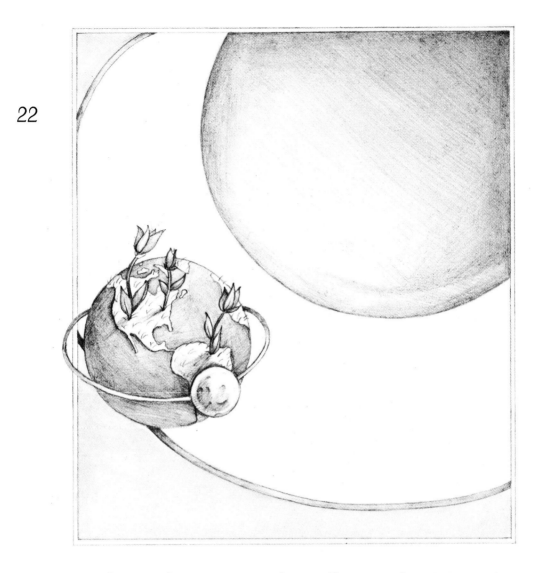

The moon's gravity wins the small game, when it is tugging against the ocean. But earth's gravity holds the moon itself. Earth is so much bigger that its gravity keeps the moon from drifting off into space. In fact, if the moon weren't moving around the earth, it would crash into it.

The sun is many times more massive than earth. The sun's gravity pulls on earth the same way earth's pulls on the moon.

The sun holds the earth in an elliptical (oval) path. If it didn't, Earth would move off into space. All living things would die from the cold. Gravity keeps that from happening.

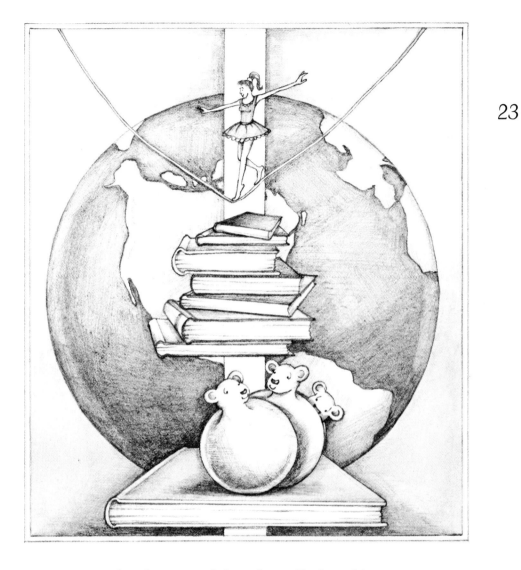

Newton also discovered that the pull of earth's gravity comes from the very center of the earth. Gravity always pulls from the most massive central spot.

Every object has a center of gravity. If a pile of books gets too heavy on one side, it starts to topple over. "Bop-em" toys stay up, because their center of gravity is at the base. As long as tightrope walkers in a circus keep their center of gravity right over the rope, they can't fall. But if they tip too far to one side or the other, even for a second, down they go! Gravity pulls from center to center.

Isaac Newton was very sure his ideas about gravity were right. To prove them, he had to invent a whole new kind of mathematics called calculus. It took him twenty years.

Newton's math explains how the Earth and the planets move. Using calculus even helped scientists to discover two new planets, too small to see without a telescope. Observers could tell the planets existed, because their gravity was changing the motion of other planets. They finally spotted Neptune and Pluto when calculus told them where to look.

Everyone—from astronomers (who study the stars) to builders to astronauts to circus stars—uses Newton's discoveries. But Newton didn't discover everything about gravity. He couldn't explain exactly how it works.

About eighty years ago, another young man, working in an office in Switzerland, did some thinking about gravity. Albert Einstein didn't need a laboratory, because he didn't like to experiment. Einstein liked to think.

Einstein described how gravity can bend space and turn straight lines into curves. It can even attract light. Many of Einstein's ideas are so difficult that the average person can't understand them. Most of the time, it doesn't matter.

Einstein's special discoveries about gravity matter only when gravity is super-strong. Earth's gravity is too weak to bend light. But the sun and certain stars have gravities strong enough to curve space. They can bend the light coming from stars behind them, enough for scientists to measure. Careful experiments always show that Einstein is right.

The strongest gravity may belong to a black hole in space. A black hole's gravity is so powerful, no light can escape from it. That's why it looks black. Scientists know black holes are there because they curve the space around them.

Scientists think black holes might be stars that have collapsed. Gravity squeezes all their mass into a small ball, the way you might squeeze fresh bread into a heavy lump. The earth is too small ever to become a black hole, but if it could, it would have to collapse down to the size of a marble.

Einstein's ideas about gravity help astronomers to study faraway stars and physicists to understand motion and astronauts to plan space travel. But not even Einstein could say exactly how gravity works.

Gravity rules the universe. It keeps everything in place, from the largest star to the smallest rock.

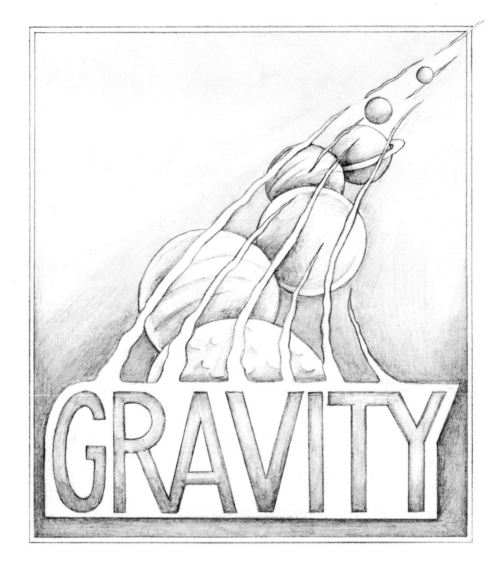

Other forces in the universe, such as electricity, magnetism, and the forces that hold atoms together are all much stronger than the force of gravity, but they have to be close to what they are working on, to work at all. Gravity can pull over billions of miles, even though its force gets weaker and weaker as objects get farther apart.

These other forces can push as well as pull. Magnets sometimes push each other away, and static electricity can make the hairs on your head stand apart. Gravity is like a one-way street. It only pulls.

Many scientists think gravity works through invisible particles called *gravitons*. Gravitons could carry energy between objects, pulling them together.

No one has ever seen a graviton. No one even knows for sure if they exist. If they do, it will take another special scientist, like Galileo or Newton or Einstein, to find and explain them. Then, perhaps everyone will understand exactly how gravity works. And why "up" is up.